# The Little Red Notebook

A Parent's **Safe Space** to Write Down Thoughts and Anger Issues; Have Clarity and Gain Control over Emotions for a Peaceful Mind and Calmness

## Sometimes, all you need is someone who will listen.

So consider this notebook as your personal therapist, a safe space for you to rant, to write down all your hurt, frustrations, and helplessness. A place for you to just let it all out.

And once you are done, take a deep breath, cry if you need to, and remember that you'll be okay, that this is just a passing moment where you feel overwhelmed and exhausted.

Anger is a complex emotion and you should commit to working on yourself. And this is how you can start. Remember that Anger Management is a skill and the first step to master it is becoming aware of how and why you got angry, finding your triggers and being aware of the patterns. This is where this notebook comes in.

It is okay to express what you feel so you will be able to let them go right after. What is not okay is to dwell in those feelings. Please use this notebook as a means to release the anger and gain calmness. Once you have a more peaceful mind, take some time to read your words and ask yourself these questions:

- Identify your trigger: I got angry because?
- Identify the feeling behind your anger. Are you hurt? Frustrated?
  -I feel ─────────────
- Why did you get angry?
- What do you think others felt when you got angry?

Then take another deep breath to regain yourself. It sounds simple but it takes time to master this. But we know you can do it!

Thank you for choosing The Little Red Notebook as your companion on this journey. We're grateful to be a part of your emotional wellness journey.

With empathy and understanding,

*Vivian Foster*

)